0 01 01 0840036 6

E974.9 Cam
Cameron, Eileen.
G is for Garden State :
a New Jersey alphabet

 **W9-BBA-358**

JUL 3 0 2004

G is for Garden State

A New Jersey Alphabet

Written by Eileen Cameron and Illustrated by Doris Ettlinger

The original sculpture of Haddy by John Giannotti was used as reference for the "R" painting.

Special thanks to Lenape historians, John and Herbert Kraft, and to the staffs of the National Parks at Morristown, Edison and the Statue of Liberty, the Franklin Mineral Museum, The Philadelphia Academy of Natural Sciences, the New Jersey State Museum at Trenton, Rutgers' Cook College and Port Norris, and the New Jersey State Departments of Agriculture, Commerce, Division of Fish and Wildlife, and the State Library.
—Eileen Cameron

Thanks to Edward F. Norton, Jr. of the Muralo Paint Company, Capt. Roy P. Wood, Jr. of the Sandy Hook Pilots, Laura McDonald and children, John Giannotti, Morgan Kinney, Patricia Thiede, and Emi.
—Doris Ettlinger

Sleeping Bear Press
310 North Main Street, Suite 300
Chelsea, MI 48118
www.sleepingbearpress.com

THOMSON
GALE

© Thomson Gale, a part of the Thomson Corporation. Thomson and Star Logo are trademarks and Gale and Sleeping Bear Press are registered trademarks used herein under license.

Printed and bound in Canada.

10 9 8 7 6 5 4 3 2 1

Library of Congress Cataloging-in-Publication Data

Cameron, Eileen.
G is for Garden State : a New Jersey alphabet / written by Eileen Cameron ; illustrated by Doris Ettlinger.
p. cm.
ISBN 1-58536-152-6
1. New Jersey—Juvenile literature. 2. English language—Alphabet—Juvenile literature. [1. New Jersey. 2. Alphabet.] I. Ettlinger, Doris, ill. II. Title.
F134.3.C25 2004
974.9—dc22   2003025873

To my parents, and to all the Kirwins, Knowleses, and O'Loughlins,
for love of history and literature, and to my family "advisors,"
Rosie, Jean, Tom, Peter, Michael, and Mary.

EILEEN

❧

To my neighbors on Imlaydale Road.

DORIS

The Lenape, who were Native Americans and known as Woodland Indians, lived in New Jersey for thousands of years before the Europeans settled here.

Green forests and fertile fields provided shelter and game for the hunter with bow and arrow as well as nuts and berries for the gatherer with baskets. New Jersey is a peninsula and the Lenape had access to fresh and salt waters where they fished with nets and dug for clams.

Wonderful sounds inherited from the Native Americans sing in the names of our lakes, towns, and rivers—Absecon, Hackensack, Musconetcong, Hopatcong, Raritan, Navesink, Nantuxent, Piscataway, Tuckahoe, and Passaic.

A is for Arrowhead
carved by the Lenape,
who used arrowheads to hunt for meat
and nets for fishing in the sea.

B is for Boardwalk
down at the shore,
where children bike and play,
and mewing seagulls soar.

Boardwalks are built along the beach in many New Jersey shore towns. Visitors watch the sea, stroll, jog, and bike. Amusement piers feature rides on roller coasters and merry-go-rounds. Cotton candy and saltwater taffy are traditions.

The first boardwalk was built in Atlantic City in 1870 so people would not track sand into the hotels. The board game, Monopoly, is based on Atlantic City. The most expensive property in Monopoly is Boardwalk.

C is for Cranberries,
bright, red berries for
Thanksgiving dinner,
served in a sauce
for a holiday winner.

Cranberries have grown in the Pinelands for centuries. They are a New World plant and Native Americans used the wild berries for food. Early English settlers enjoyed tart cranberry sauce with venison and turkey.

Cranberries grow in low-lying areas called bogs. Blueberries, grown on low shrubs, are also cultivated in the Pinelands. Elizabeth White of Whitesbog developed and marketed the first cultivated blueberries in 1916.

New Jersey ranks third in the production of cranberries in the United States and second in blueberries. The blueberry is the state fruit of New Jersey.

D is for Dogs.
Trainers teach them to go and to stay.
Smart dogs guide sight-impaired people.
Seeing Eye Dogs show them the way.

The Seeing Eye was founded in 1929 and moved to Morristown in 1931. It was the first guide dog training center in the country.

Seeing Eye dogs are trained to be the "eyes" for the blind people they guide. Trainers work with their dogs in the stores and on the sidewalks of Morristown, teaching them to guide their new masters safely through the aisles and across the streets. They teach the dogs skills to help their owners travel independently and with dignity.

The Seeing Eye breeds German shepherds, and Labrador and golden retrievers to be companion guide dogs.

E e

E is for Thomas Edison,
for until he turned on the lights,
the world lived
in long, dark nights.

Thomas Edison, who lived and worked in New Jersey, was one of the greatest inventors of the nineteenth century. He transformed how people lived by developing the electric light bulb in 1879 in Menlo Park. He also devised a system to deliver electricity to homes and businesses by building the first electric power plant so people could have lights and machines powered by electricity. Roselle, New Jersey, was the first town to be lighted by electricity.

Edison often worked 20 hours a day developing inventions to make life easier and more enjoyable. At his labs in Menlo Park and West Orange he invented many firsts including the phonograph and the movie projector. He held over one thousand patents.

Thriving iron mines functioned in colonial New Jersey. In the 1800s glassworks hummed in the Pinelands. Water powered factories in Paterson, one of the first planned industrial cities, is where the mills made textiles. The twentieth century saw the production of ships, motors, and electrical equipment.

Currently New Jersey leads the United States in manufacturing petrochemicals, plastics, medicines and pharmaceuticals, and electrical goods and machines. The Mars Company in Hackettstown makes the colorful chocolate M & M candies.

In early days sailing ships transported goods. Later trains carried the products. Today container ships, airplanes, and trucks that use a modern highway system take the goods to market.

Ff

F is for Factories,
where people work as teams,
making useful things for us
with busy, whirring machines.

New Jersey is called the Garden State because of the many gardens here. Fertile land and abundant water make farming flourish. Even though New Jersey is the most densely populated state, having the most people per square mile, it is a leading producer of agricultural products.

Greenhouses and nurseries, dairy and vegetable farms are important. Major crops include tomatoes, corn, asparagus, eggplant, peaches, and berries. New Jersey produce is shipped widely throughout the United States and Canada. Many homes have vegetable gardens and flower gardens, some of which are like bowers, shaded by trees or arbors.

The honeybee, New Jersey's state insect, helps fruits and vegetables to grow by pollinating the plants. Formal flower gardens beautify the state. In spring, cherry blossoms glow in Branch Brook Park in Newark, tulips at Skylands, and two thousand varieties of irises in the Presby Garden in Montclair.

G is for Gardens
that fill the state's bowers
with color and fragrance,
farm vegetables, and flowers.

H is for the Highlands,
the beautiful green hills,
covered with parks and forests,
lakes, streams, and rills.

The Highlands is a large region of mountains, lakes, reservoirs, farms, and forests in northwest New Jersey. Rivers, streams, and small brooks, known as rills, flow down the area's water channels. The region supplies drinking water to 50 percent of the state.

An ice age glacier created many of the lakes in the area while others were man-made. Lake Mohawk and Lake Hopatcong are two of the biggest lakes nestled in the ridges of the mountains. Skiers, campers, hikers, and boaters use the waters and trails here.

H is also for High Point State Park which occupies the highest location above sea level in the state. The Appalachian Trail runs through the park.

I is for Inventors
like Vail and Morse,
who sent messages by wire,
by telegraph, of course!

1948
SELMAN WAXMAN
ALBERT SCHATZ

Streptomycin

1870

Adhesive
Bandages
ROBERT JOHNSON
GEORGE SEABURY

1877

Phonograph
THOMAS EDISON

1904
Ice Cream Cone
ITALO
MARCHIONY

Telegraph
ALFRED
VAIL

1838

New Jersey has been at the hub of research for more than a hundred years, with scientists thinking of new and better ways to do things. In 1811 John Stevens developed the world's first steam ferry line. In 1838 Samuel Morse and Alfred Vail perfected the electromagnetic telegraph in Morristown so people could send messages swiftly over great distances. Robert Johnson and George Seabury introduced the BAND-AID® in 1870.

John Holland built the first practical submarine, launching a trial sub in the Passaic River in 1878. He sold the United States Navy its first submarine in 1900. Holland used an electric engine underwater and a gasoline engine on the surface.

In 1948 scientists at Bell Laboratories developed the transistor and in 1962 the first telecommunications satellite. Albert Einstein, the great scientist, worked at Princeton University.

Today New Jersey remains important in high tech research, including medicine, computers, and telecommunications.

Ii

New Jersey, a colony of England, was named after Jersey, one of the Channel Islands in the English Channel. One of the original colonies, New Jersey was the third to sign the United States Constitution in 1787, becoming the third state of the new Union.

Two United States presidents hailed from New Jersey. Grover Cleveland, the twenty-second and twenty-fourth president was born in Caldwell and was president twice, taking office in 1885 and 1893. Woodrow Wilson was president of Princeton University and governor of New Jersey. He became the twenty-eighth president, serving from 1913 to 1921.

The battleship *New Jersey*, named for our state, is now a museum in Camden.

New Jersey's state seal on the state flag features a shield. On the shield are three plows which represent agriculture, and two goddesses depicting the state motto, "Liberty and Prosperity." A horse is also pictured on the shield. Horses were important for farms. Today, horse farms are a large industry in New Jersey. The horse is the state animal.

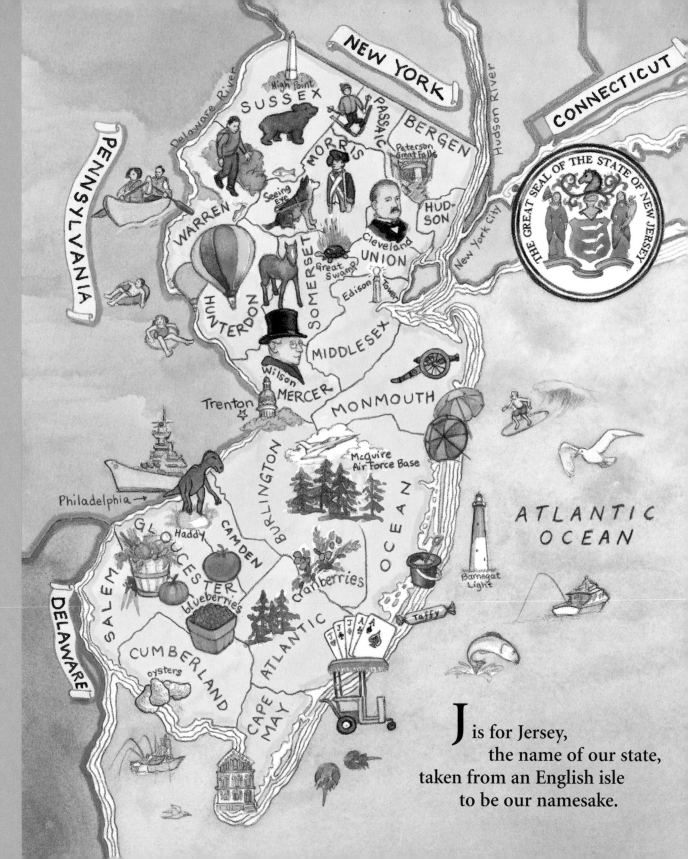

J is for Jersey,
the name of our state,
taken from an English isle
to be our namesake.

K is for the Knobbed Whelk,
　　　spiraled treasure on the shore,
　　hold it to your ear
　　　　　and hear the ocean roar.

The Knobbed Whelk is the state shell of New Jersey. It is a large, yellow-gray shell with a cream to red opening. It is also known as a conch shell and can be discovered on most bays and beaches. Whelks are harvested for food which is often canned.

Periwinkles, scallops, slipper shells, moon snails, wentletraps, and clam shells can also be found on the beaches of the shore.

Liberty State Park is located in Jersey City on New York Bay across from New York City, the Statue of Liberty on Liberty Island, and Ellis Island and the Museum of Immigration. The park has a museum and marina. Ferryboats take park visitors out to Liberty Island and the statue, which is within New York's jurisdiction.

The Statue of Liberty was a gift from France to the United States and has been a beacon of welcome to new immigrants arriving in New York Harbor for over a hundred years. Adjacent to the park and its piers is the Liberty Science Center which features exhibits on technology, inventions, and the environment.

L is for Liberty State Park
overlooking New York Bay,
and the Lady who welcomes
freedom lovers on their way.

Ll

M is for Molly Pitcher,
colonial patriot,
who carried water to the soldiers
because they were hot.

Legends say that Molly Hayes, heroine of the Battle of Monmouth, was the wife of an American soldier in the Continental Army. On the very hot day of June 28, 1778, as the American troops were battling the British at Monmouth, New Jersey, Molly risked her life by carrying pitchers of water to the soldiers manning the cannons.

When her husband fell wounded, she took his place at the gun and continued to fire on the British, helping General Washington and the Americans to a major victory. She became known as Molly Pitcher.

m
M

New Jersey's peninsula has many sheltered ports on the Atlantic Ocean and Delaware River. The Lenape first used the state's waterways and harbors. In colonial times there was a whaling industry off Cape May. Through the eighteenth and nineteenth centuries ships carried products from New Jersey farms. Shipbuilding and fishing industries prospered.

Today, Ports Newark and Elizabeth, with New York, form one of the largest shipping and container ports in the world, moving cargos of chemicals and manufactured goods. Sporting navigators paddle kayaks on the lakes in the northwest mountains of New Jersey. Rafts float down the Delaware River. Canoes shoot through the rivers of the Pinelands. Sport fishing boats motor on the Atlantic Ocean, and sailboats glide on the Hudson River on the north and the Delaware Bay on the south.

N is for the Navigators
who sail from Jersey's ports,
from rivers and sea harbors,
with cargo of all sorts.

O is for Oyster
found in waters by the tide,
eaten raw on the half shell
and in hot stew or deep-fried.

O

Oysters are harvested or landed in New Jersey on the Atlantic Ocean bay areas and the Delaware Bay. Some oysters grow naturally and some grow or are cultured in managed beds. Oysters are harvested by dredging and scraping them off the beds.

New Jersey ranks in the middle of the 19 coastal states that have oyster harvesting industries. The first Americans in New Jersey to catch oysters were the Lenape. They smoked their oysters and used the shells for wampum.

O is also for Oyster Creek Access, a state wildlife management area. New Jersey protects waters and woods with state parks, forests, federal preservation areas, and over a hundred wildlife management areas. Some of these nature areas are Beaver Brook, Great Swamp, Butterfly Bog, Lizard Tail Swamp, and Mad Horse Creek.

Pp

P is for the Pinelands,
with forests of oak and pine,
berries in the bogs
and fruit upon the vine.

The Pinelands in south Jersey, also known as the Pine Barrens, covers over a million acres of wilderness with forests, cedar swamps and huge underground water sources or aquifers. Farms produce cranberries, blueberries, and other fruits and vegetables.

The Pinelands has been designated as a National Reserve for Environmental Protection. The New Jersey Pinelands Commission guides the preservation of the reserve and its deep aquifers, clean streams, and extensive pine woods. Visitors camp, kayak, and canoe.

P is also for peninsula. A peninsula is land almost completely surrounded by water. New Jersey is a peninsula bounded by the Hudson and Delaware Rivers and the Atlantic Ocean and Delaware Bay.

Quercus Alba, a 600-year-old white oak tree, stands in the historic cemetery of the Presbyterian Church in Basking Ridge. Everyone from early day Native Americans to modern children on school buses have passed by its stretching branches. It is one of the largest and oldest trees in the state. Other ancient white and red oaks grow in various parts of New Jersey. *Quercus Alba* is the Latin name for white oak.

The Red Oak is the state tree of New Jersey. *Quercus Rubra* is the Latin name for New Jersey's red oak. The red oak produces many acorns and turns a strong red in the fall.

Q also stands for Quakers, who came to America for religious freedom and settled in western New Jersey and Pennsylvania.

Q is for *Quercus Alba,*
the grand, old oak tree,
that watched over the village
through long centuries.

R is for Reptile
and New Jersey's come big and small,
but Haddy the dinosaur
was the biggest of them all.

New Jersey has many small reptiles such as the snakes and turtles that live in the woods, swamps, hills, and mountains. But in 1858 the largest reptile was unearthed in Haddonfield in an ancient seabed. It was then the most complete dinosaur skeleton found anywhere in the world. It was named *Hadrosaurus foulkii* after the discoverer, William Parker Foulke, and the site, Haddonfield. It was the first dinosaur skeleton to be mounted and displayed in public. The Philadelphia Academy of Natural Sciences continues to have an exhibit on Haddy.

Hadrosaurus foulkii is the state dinosaur. Haddy was 25 feet long, weighed about seven to ten tons, and was a plant eater.

A large sculpture of Haddy, by John Giannotti, stands in Haddonfield today.

S is for the Shore
where children love to be,
digging in the sand, surfing in the sea,
fishing from the piers, in summers filled with glee.

In the summer, Jerseyites head to "The Shore" and to the sea and its beaches and bays. Tourism, including the shore trade, is the second largest business in New Jersey. The Lenape were the first summer visitors, enjoying fishing and clamming. By the early 1800s hotels were advertising the charms of the shore to the residents of Philadelphia, Pennsylvania.

Many lighthouses guarded the coast and guided ships to safety. Sandy Hook Lighthouse has burned its steady beam since 1764 and is currently the oldest continually operating lighthouse in the country.

Cape May was one of the first American beach resorts. It hosted early "Summer White Houses" for Presidents Franklin Pierce, James Buchanan, Ulysses S. Grant, Chester Arthur, and Benjamin Harrison.

S s

Tt

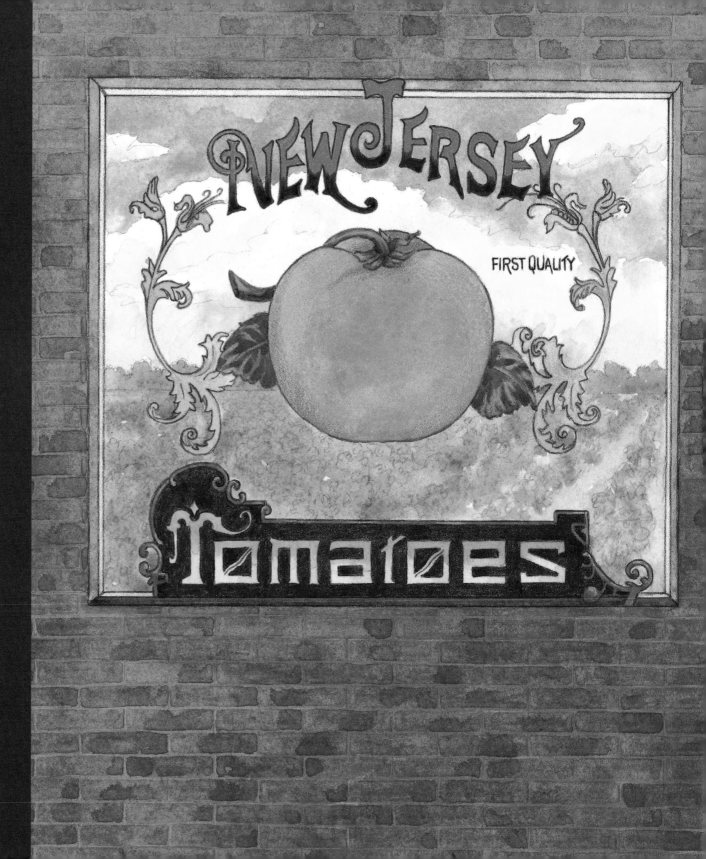

Trenton sits on the banks of the Delaware River. The governor's office is located here. The State Assembly and Senate also meet in Trenton to make state laws. Trenton is the site of the first major American victory over the British in the Revolutionary War. General Washington and the Continental troops crossed the icy Delaware River on Christmas 1776 and surprised the British.

T is also for tomatoes. New Jersey produces many varieties of this tangy, vitamin C filled fruit. Campbell's Soup Company in Camden canned tomatoes and in 1897 began to market the first-ever condensed soups. Tomato was one of the first soups sold and is still a favorite.

T is for Trenton,
capital of our state,
 and for juicy Jersey tomatoes,
 the best we ever ate!

The summer pastime of baseball had been growing as an informal game when, in 1846, a group of New Yorkers one day took the ferry across the Hudson River to the country in Hoboken. There on a New Jersey field Alexander Cartwright and his friends of the New York Knickerbocker Club played the first baseball game held under formal rules with the diamond field layout.

Another New Jersey sports first was the first football game between two colleges played by Princeton and Rutgers in New Brunswick in 1869. Rutgers was triumphant in the first game but the next week Princeton won the rematch. Now over 600 colleges and universities field football teams.

Althea Gibson of East Orange is one of the most famous sports figures from New Jersey. In 1957 she was the first African-American woman to become the Wimbledon singles tennis champion. She also won the U.S. Open and French Open tennis titles.

U is for Umpires
who call to New Jersey players all,
to signal the summer's game beginning
with the grand command—"Play Ball!"

V

V is for the Violet,
little flower in purple dress,
sunning on the greening bank,
a welcome springtime guest.

The violet is New Jersey's state flower. Its perky face graces stream banks, edges of meadows, and woods in the spring. It is often found near pink and white spring beauties and yellow dog-toothed violets.

In spring, summer, and fall wildflowers flourish by roadside, field, and woods. Buttercups and daisies are followed in high summer by blue chicory flowers and white Queen Ann's lace, and then purple asters and goldenrod of fall.

Purple pickerel weed grows in Great Swamp, beach goldenrod by the hollies at Sandy Hook Seashore, rhododendrons at High Point State Park, and the multi-flora rose by the marshes of Cape May.

George Washington, the Commander of the Continental Army from 1775 to 1783, led the Americans to victory and freedom. General Washington and the troops fought numerous battles during the Revolutionary War in New Jersey. He was a leader of integrity and vision who became the first president and helped establish our democracy.

Washington camped in many places in the state. He and the troops spent two harsh winters in Morristown. He wrote his 1783 farewell speech to the troops while at Rockingham in Rocky Hill. Places named for him here include seven towns; parks named Washington's Rock in Greenbrook, Washington's Headquarters in Morristown, and Washington's Crossing on the Delaware; a garden in New Vernon; and the great bridge that spans the Hudson River.

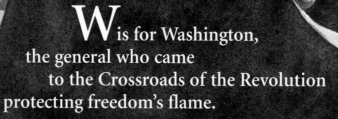

W is for Washington,
the general who came
to the Crossroads of the Revolution
protecting freedom's flame.

X is for the Crossroads of Migration
over the beach and the bay,
where millions of migrating birds
pause to eat and rest and play.

In the fall millions of birds flying from north to south, and in the spring flying south to north, cross over New Jersey on the route called the Atlantic Flyway. Ocean and bay areas on the east coast offer food and rest. Birds needing woodland and river habitats fly on the pathway over the Delaware River area on the west.

New Jersey is also known as the Crossroads of the Revolution. The Continental Army clashed with the enemy in more engagements in New Jersey than in any other state. New Jersey was located between the British stronghold of New York and colonial-held Philadelphia. The state also offered safe encampments, iron mines, forges, and munitions to General Washington.

Y is for the Yellow Goldfinch,
   agile bird flying free,
   bounding like a stunt plane,
   calling "toHEE, toHEE, toHEE."

Yy

The goldfinch is the official state bird of New Jersey. This bright yellow bird can be seen darting about fields, meadows, and open woods. It likes to feed and nest near the ground.

Goldfinches eat weed seeds, wild fruit, and sometimes caterpillars. They especially like thistle seeds and sunflower seeds and will eat at winter feeders stocked with these seeds. They do not usually migrate and stay in New Jersey all year.

Z is for Zinc,
dug from our mines,
and used to cover metals,
it's called to galvanize!

Zinc was mined at the Franklin Mine in Sussex County, from the mid 1800s to 1954. This mine was considered to be one of the richest zinc mines in the world. Zinc is used to cover other metals such as iron and steel to prevent corrosion or rusting. The process of covering or plating with zinc is called galvanizing.

Zinc has many other manufacturing uses. Some include the use of zinc oxide, which helps make rubber tires stronger and which is used as a component in salves and lotions.

The U.S. "copper" penny is actually 97.5 percent zinc and is plated or covered with 2.5 percent copper. Iron was mined in the Pinelands and in northwest New Jersey beginning in the 1700s. The Stirling Hill Mining Museum and the Franklin Mineral Museum tell the story of mining in New Jersey.

Zz

A Garden Full of Facts

1. What bodies of water border New Jersey, making it a peninsula?

2. What ancient reptile found in New Jersey ate plants and was 30 feet long?

3. Where in New Jersey was there a presidential "Summer White House"?

4. What is the Latin name for New Jersey's state tree?

5. Who, with his colonial troops, commanded a boat across a dangerous, ice-filled river to fight and bring us freedom?

6. What two red fruits that grow in New Jersey supply the important vitamin C?

7. How were the lakes in the northwest mountains formed?

8. Who changed how people read books at night?

9. How are the products that are manufactured in New Jersey packed and moved by water overseas?

10. Colonists from England, Holland, and Sweden named many New Jersey towns and waterways. Who gave Hopatcong and Navesink their names?

11. What type of research do the many scientists working in New Jersey do?

12. Where was the first practical submarine tested?

13. What New Jersey first makes hotel keepers happy?

14. Where did New Jersey get its name, and what is its nickname?

15. Who was the New Jersey woman who researched and developed the blueberry to be a marketable fruit?

16. What visitors to the Jersey Shore find much-needed food and rest before continuing their journeys north and south by air?

17. In the 1800s New Jersey factories made different types of threads and cloth. What kind of products do our factories make now?

18. What fruits and vegetables are important farm crops in New Jersey?

19. Water is an important commodity for the state's towns and cities. What area supplies 50 percent of the water used by New Jersey residents?

20. Little League and school teams play many baseball games here. Where was the first official game of baseball played?

Answers

1. The Atlantic Ocean, Delaware Bay, Hudson River, and Delaware River

2. *Hadrosaurus foulkii,* or "Haddy"

3. Cape May

4. *Quercus rubra;* formerly *Quercus borealis maxima* was preferred.

5. General Washington

6. Cranberries and tomatoes

7. By glacier and man-made

8. Thomas Edison

9. Goods are packed in truck-sized containers and loaded on large container ships.

10. Native Americans—the Lenape

11. Research in medicines, computers, and telecommunications

12. Passaic River

13. Boardwalks

14. Jersey is the name of an English Channel Island. New Jersey is also known as the Garden State.

15. Elizabeth White

16. Migrating birds

17. Chemicals, plastics, electrical goods, and medicines

18. Corn, asparagus, eggplant, tomatoes, peaches, and berries

19. The Highlands

20. Hoboken

Eileen Cameron

Eileen Cameron is an involved preservationist who is interested in protecting our natural and historical resources. She serves on the boards of the Washington Association of New Jersey at Morristown National Historical Park and the Life Guard Board of George Washington's Mount Vernon, Virginia. She has served on her local zoning board and the environmental commission. She holds degrees from Skidmore College and New York University and published her first children's book, *Canyon*, in 2002.

Eileen grew up in Chatham and now lives in New Vernon, New Jersey, by the Great Swamp and Loantaka Park where she watches the wild ducks, geese, and great blue herons, and near Morristown where the Continental Army camped during the Revolutionary War.

Doris Ettlinger

Doris Ettlinger was born on Staten Island, New York, and graduated from the Rhode Island School of Design. She has been illustrating professionally ever since. She tells her art students that drawing every day improves her skills, just as practicing an instrument improves a musician's skills or working out improves an athlete's performance.

Doris lives and works in a 150-year-old gristmill in western New Jersey with her husband, two teenagers, and a Welsh corgi. She says her characters often look like the eight-year-old Doris who still hangs out inside her "mature" self.